Set your house in order

Personal or Small Group Study Manual

Mark Lloydbottom

e: info@yourmoneycounts.org.uk   w: www.yourmoneycounts.org.uk
YourMoneyCountsUK   @YMC_UK

Copyright @2019 by Your Money Counts

All rights reserved.

ISBN: 978-1-908423-26-9

Published by Your Money Counts, UK.

Unless otherwise stated, Scripture quotations are from the Holy Bible, New International Version – UK copyright © 1973, 1978, 1984 by the International Bible Society.

Please note:
This study cannot in any shape or form be regarded as advice. In taking any action following on from reading Set Your House in Order it is important to state that the student of this study should seek proper professional advice. No responsibility can be accepted by the author or Your Money Counts in respect of any actions taken or refrained from.

Designed by: Loulita Gill

> This workbook belongs to:
>
> ....
>
> and is personal and confidential. *Please return to me and kindly do not look past this page.*

Foreword

It is a known fact that retirement and death are two life realities that we least enjoy talking about and are mostly ill-prepared for.

Of unfathomable comfort to the Christian is the truth that both of these have been fully covered and provided for in the death and resurrection of the Lord Jesus Christ.

I find these words of His most comforting:

"Therefore, do not worry about tomorrow, for tomorrow will worry about itself. Each day has enough trouble of its own"; and "In my Father's house are many rooms; if it were not so, I would have told you. I am going there to prepare a place for you. And if I go and prepare a place for you, I will come back and take you to be with me that you also may be where I am. You know the way to the place to where I am going" Matthew 6:34 and John 14:2-4.

These great promises, however, do not mean that we must ignore our responsibility of planning for the future so that we honour God in the way we prepare for the realities of retirement and death.

This study written by my dear friend and brother in Christ, Mark Lloydbottom, is a worthy addition to the Your Money Counts range of books and studies and will assist you in preparing for these life realities.

Estate planning and preparing a Will can be a daunting task and this study will be of tremendous help to you because it is biblically based and written in Mark's usual sensitive, yet direct style.

I commend it to you and pray that God will be honoured and His Kingdom extended through the decisions taken and actions arising from your participation in this study.

Grace and peace
Billy Nield
Cape Town, South Africa

NOTES OF THANKS FROM MARK LLOYDBOTTOM

My thanks to Billy for his friendship and kind words. He is a lay preacher and Senior Partner of one of the global accounting firms. In this capacity I have no doubt that Billy has advised on estate planning many mores than I.

I also wish to place on record my thanks to Stuart Palmer for his comprehensive editing and also Margaret Thornton who was formerly Head of Probate at Baldwins Group for her editing of some of the more technical aspects of this study.

I leave my final thanks for Howard Dayton the founder of Crown Financial Ministries and Compass who has authored a range of books and studies all of which have been a source of inspiration as well as education.

Welcome

I really appreciate you investing the time you commit to this *Set Your House in Order* study.

I know from experience that attending to matters relating to death and latter year financial planning is not everyone's first choice activity. But, in my many years as the founder and then managing partner of an accountancy business I have experienced so many people in this situation; from those undertaking no end of life planning at all to those who have everything tied down and in place, ship shape, Bristol fashion.

You may be looking at this study in a small group, or on your own. If studying alone, you may wish in due course to follow on and lead a *Setting Your House In Order* small group and discuss these important matters with others in your church.

It is important to give due thought and consideration to his or her financial and estate planning and decide what actions to take. Procrastination, putting off doing anything, is all too common. There are many reasons for this. Some are unwilling to face the fact that we will all one day 'graduate' and feel that planning for their death forces then to acknowledge this. Others feel they have too little to be bothered with or that they simply cannot find the time to address the issue of planning when they are unlikely to die for years yet.

One common reason for not taking action is that couples find it hard to agree what to do. That is often the case for those who have children from an earlier marriage - a blended family. One spouse might feel it is *their* children who should inherit *their* wealth and not those of the current spouse. Thus, money can become a marital problem and, in order to avoid arguments, they ignore the issue leaving it to be sorted out, by others, after they die as an easy way out of this conundrum.

YOUR MONEY COUNTS RESOURCES

We have a range of books and studies that enable you to study further what the Bible has to say about handling your money and possessions. Our overview of biblical finance can be found in *Bought*. This book is available online and provides an essential overview for gaining a better understanding of what the Bible has to say about this important subject.

NAVIGATING YOUR FINANCES GOD'S WAY

On the yourmoneycounts.org website you will find our FREE 5-part online training programme that looks at a whole range of financial planning matters from a biblical perspective.

The Bible encourages us to set our house in order and become organised in our planning. I would encourage you to take your planning forward so that it is documented, completed and implemented.

The biblical starting point for this study can be found in:

Isaiah 38:1
"In those days Hezekiah was sick and near death. And Isaiah the prophet, the son of Amoz, went to him and said to him, 'Thus says the Lord: 'Set your house in order, for you shall die and not live'" (NKJV).

1 Corinthians 14:33
"...for God is not a God of confusion" (WEB).

1 Corinthians 14:40
"But everything should be done in a fitting and orderly way."

You may recall Benjamin Franklin's maxim that "failing to plan, is planning to fail."

And, permit me to end this welcome with a word of [biblical] observation from Isaiah 55: 8-9: "For my thoughts are not your thoughts, neither are your ways my ways,' declares the Lord. 'As the heavens are higher than the earth, so are my ways higher than your ways and my thoughts than your thoughts."

It would have been possible to have made this study much longer. But, I understand that for many this is not an easy subject to address. For that reason I have sought to only include only those matters that I consider essential.

So, without further ado please start your journey. We pray that you will be informed, encouraged and blessed as you work your way through this study.

Mark Lloydbottom

Mark Lloydbottom, FCA
Founder, Your Money Counts, UK

Table of contents

8	**CHAPTER 1: GETTING STARTED**
8	Overview for the study group leader
8	Overview for the participant
9	Our study objectives
9	Case study 1
12	Contentment
12	Homework
12	Practical Application 1: Organising your documents
14	**CHAPTER 2: STEWARDSHIP BASICS**
14	End times planning is a challenge for so many
15	God owns everything
16	We are all stewards
16	Seek counsel
17	Homework
18	Practical Application 2: Deed of ownership
19	Practical Application 3: List of advisors
21	**CHAPTER 3: LOOKING AT FAMILY AND THE FUTURE**
21	Case study 2
22	The Bible on worry
22	Providing for the family
23	The worries and dangers that can arise with debt
23	An eye on the future
24	Homework
24	Practical Application 4: Future income needs
24	Practical Application 5: Insurance cover
24	Practical Application 6: Over insured?
25	Practical Application 7: Lasting power of attorney
25	Practical Application 8: Letter of wishes
26	Practical Application 9: guardians for children
26	Practical Application 10: Letter to children/grandchildren
27	Practical Application 11: Your Will
28	Whereabouts of documents to register your death and obtain probate
29	Reasons for updating an existing Will
30	**CHAPTER 4: LEGACY PLANNING**
30	Sharing your journey
31	Inheritances
32	Generosity
33	Planning lessons from Abraham's family
34	About leaving an inheritance
34	Case study 3
36	Homework
36	Practical Application 12: Personal legacy
36	Practical Application 13: Funeral instructions
37	Practical Application 14: Testimony letter
37	Dying without a Will or without a valid Will
38	Intestacy rules
39	Case study 4
39	Case study 5
40	Why people don't make a Will
40	Distribution of personal property
41	A note to the main breadwinner
43	Summary of your actions
44	**APPENDIX**
44	Technical terms explained
47	Your documents
48	List of advisors
49	Funeral instructions
50	Distribution of personal property
51	Some thoughts on inheritance tax planning

Chapter 1:
Getting Started

OVERVIEW FOR THE STUDY GROUP LEADER

One of the objectives for this first study is to begin to develop close relationships among those participating and to begin your group discussions.

Ask each participant to introduce themselves - maybe taking five minutes each. Ask them to share how they came to faith in Jesus Christ, what they do for a living, and something about their family. As the leader you may wish to ask supplementary questions.

Recommend: Start and end each study in prayer.

OVERVIEW FOR THE PARTICIPANT

This four-part study provides a combination of biblical references, questions, case studies, commentary, homework and practical applications. Not all of the latter will necessarily apply so decide which are your priorities and make sure you embark on this very important journey.

My objective is to combine biblical wisdom and instruction with insights and stories that will help you toward tackling an aspect of life that, for most, is so challenging.

Prepare to discover some interesting perspectives - even seasoned professional advisers have discovered this study to be of great help and value in their own planning.

This study is for all adults. Not just for those who have wealth. It is relevant for those who have a young family as well as those who are taking a long hard look at their estate planning.

Enjoy and take action.

KEY VERSE

"For my thoughts are not your thoughts, neither are your ways my ways," declares the Lord. "As the heavens are higher than the earth, so are my ways higher than your ways and my thoughts than your thoughts."

Isaiah 55: 8-9

OUR STUDY OBJECTIVES

We can plan the day ahead, the next week, the next month. Some even plan a year or more ahead. But planning for the time when you pass on from this life is rarely a task that springs to mind as being something that you might relish.

The purpose of this study is to provide a framework for considering those very aspects of life, and death, that it might be easy to defer. My hope is that in creating this relatively short study, complete with our biblical basis, that this might at least create a situation where you feel that taking action is not only necessary but also really important.

But, having said that what do you hope to learn and/or accomplish by taking this study?

CASE STUDY 1

Mary wept uncontrollably as she was struggling to come to terms with the fact that her husband was dead and had just been taken covered on a stretcher from their home by the ambulance crew. Earlier, there had been no signs of anything unusual as they had all enjoyed a family meal laughing together and sharing stories. A typical family scene as the teenage children talked about their day. John has just been to see his team play Manchester United – a great game which resulted in a win while Hannah had been clothes shopping. Mary had been tidying the house while the teenagers were out when James said he wasn't feeling too well. She could hear him snoring downstairs while she was at work in the bedrooms.

But that happy family occasion was not to last much longer.

With tears flowing freely Mary, Hannah and John sat around their living room. This was just a truly awful moment in their lives. There was no describing how they all felt as this was just simply uncharted territory as they were gathered together in a sense of unbelief and denial that James was no longer with them. "No, we can't have lost Dad," sobbed Hannah while John just sat there unable to express anything. How could this have happened so suddenly? There were just no warning signs at all.

"How are you?" asked Tim. It seemed as though time had stood still for the last 24 hours as he sat there with the family still in a state of shock. Uncle Tim had travelled down from Scotland as soon as he had heard the news. He appeared calm at first but soon that facade changed, and he too was caught up in a room where tears were once again flowing freely.

After a cup of tea, the family had seemingly cried all the tears that their ducts would allow, and they sat around while Uncle Tim asked a few questions.

"Were there any signs that James was unwell?" Tim asked.
Not really was the general consensus. He was his usual cheerful self during the day, maybe a little quieter than usual."

"When did you first sense there was a problem with my brother?"

"Well, he had complained of a few chest pains in the early evening and took himself off to bed just after the 10 o'clock news having made a few comments about being fed up having to listen to politicians and some pretty sad television reports all the time. Then about 1 o'clock he woke me up saying he had some really sharp pains. I was worried – very worried and did not know what to do. So, we talked and all the time I could see he was suffering and in pain." At that point Mary's seemingly calm exterior was broken and for 15 minutes she again sobbed while the children put their arms around her and gave her hug after hug.

"I'm sorry Tim," Mary whispered.

"Not at all," was Tim's sympathetic and understanding response.

Hannah left the room to make coffee – she remembered that Uncle Tim liked his coffee black, strong and with one sugar. The refreshments, accompanied by a plate of chocolate digestive biscuits seemed to help the family calm down although Tim was acutely aware that tears were never very far from the surface.

The children had been accustomed to Uncle Tim's visits. He usually had a meal with the family early evening and then after dessert Dad and Uncle Tim would retreat to the study. They never really knew what happened between Uncle Tim and Dad except that the next morning Dad joked over the table that Uncle Tim had left with another fistful of cheques. Tim was a financial advisor in the Scottish borders and had been James' advisor for so long as the children could remember. So, when Uncle Tim enquired if he could ask Mary some questions Hannah and John exchanged glances and decided it was perhaps better that they excuse themselves and leave Mum and Uncle Tim to chat.

"I know this is such a very difficult time and I really don't wish to add to your distress, but may I just ask a few questions?"

"Yes, by all means Tim," was Mary's quavering response.

"Funeral plans – any thoughts?"

After five minutes of outpouring Mary said, "Not many it's not something we talked about – we both envisaged that we would live way beyond retirement years – James was just so young – too young to die"

"Funeral director?"

"There is one in the village we could ask," Mary offered wishing to make an attempt at answering Tim's question.

"The service, hymns? – What do you think James would have wanted?"

"No idea."

"Readings – any thoughts?"

"Again, I don't know. Oh, dear I'm not doing very well, am I?" Mary sobbed.

"Don't worry," Tim said quietly. "You will need to choose a coffin and casket. Also, who needs to know what has happened and be invited to the funeral service? The post funeral reception?"

At this point Tim realised that important as these matters were he was unlikely to make much progress with any funeral planning. He was thankful that he had persuaded his brother to sign his Will – for over 22 years he had tried to persuade James to sign even though he always came up with excuses for not signing.

James had a number of business interests and Tim had helped him put in place a number of insurance policies to cover his death so that his fellow directors would be able to buy the shares he held in the company he had founded some 16 years previously. James had always listened to his brother but didn't always take heed of the counsel he received.

1. James' family had no idea what plans they should make for the funeral as they had never really thought much about it. Have you ever talked with anyone about funeral plans? Do you think this is important and, if so, why?

Isaiah 38:1
"In those days Hezekiah was sick and near death. And Isaiah the prophet, the son of Amoz, went to him and said to him, 'Thus says the Lord: 'Set your house in order, for you shall die and not live' " (NKJV).

2. What does this verse communicate about the importance of looking at your end of life planning?

Isaiah 55: 8-9
"For my thoughts are not your thoughts, neither are your ways my ways," declares the Lord. "As the heavens are higher than the earth, so are my ways higher than your ways and my thoughts than your thoughts."

3. What does this verse communicate? Based on this passage do you think that God's financial principles will differ from how most people handle money?

4. If you have done our other biblically-based courses, what was the most helpful information you learned from reading *Your Money Counts* or watching the *Navigating Your Finances God's Way* online training, and what practical principles can you apply in this area?

SET YOUR HOUSE IN ORDER

HOW THIS STUDY IS GOING TO BE DIFFERENT
The way most people handle money stands in sharp contrast to God's financial principles. God's economy differs greatly from man's economy. The most significant difference between the two is that the Bible reveals God desires to be closely involved with your finances. Many people fail to recognise this because He has chosen to be invisible to us and to operate in the unseen, supernatural world. The world seeks to persuade us to "buy because you deserve it" and as a result many people overspend and debt levels increase. Paul tells us in 1 Timothy 6:6 that "Godliness with contentment is great gain". This is echoed again in Hebrews 13:5, "Keep your lives free from the love of money and be content with what you have, because God has said, 'Never will I leave you; never will I forsake you.'"

CONTENTMENT
1 Timothy 6:8
"If we have food and clothing with these we shall be content."

Hebrews 13:5
"Keep your life free from the love of money and be content with what you have; for He has said, 'I will never leave you or forsake you.'"

5. What does it mean to you to be content? To what extent is this dependent on how much money you have?

HOMEWORK – SESSION 1

PRACTICAL APPLICATION 1: ORGANISING YOUR DOCUMENTS
I encountered one situation where a client who was the Chairman of one of the UK's largest construction companies had died and I took up my role as executor. I started a massive sorting and tidying exercise and recall that I managed to fill five large garden refuse bags with unnecessary out of date paperwork. It took a day and a half to sort out all the paperwork and that was before I started on my main executorship responsibilities.

So, your first moment for consideration – are your papers and files in order? Do you know where everything is – does your executor know?

Here is a list of possibly relevant documents that you might have in your document filing system. Select as applicable to your circumstances:

Bank or Building Society accounts - including log in and passwords
Birth certificate
Car registration certificate
Citizenship papers
Company shareholders (or business) agreements
Debt papers e.g. loans; hire purchase, leasing
Deeds for properties
Divorce decree
Funeral wishes including invitees, service preferences

Insurance policies
Investments including Premium Bonds; shares; ISAs, securitised investments etc.
Lasting power of attorney including health and welfare
Leases
Letter of Wishes
Marriage certificate
Mortgage(s)
National insurance details
Online files, including location, filing protocol, user name and passwords
Passport
Pension policies
Professional advisors - details and what they advise you on
Retirement papers – not covered by any other point on this list
Schedule of assets
Self-assessment tax returns or any HMRC papers
Trusts
User names and passwords (all - very important)
Wills including any deeds of variation and the location of the original

NOTES

1. Some of the above may not be appropriate but I am sure you can work them out according to your own circumstances.
2. Original documents should be your first choice but failing that then a photocopy.
3. To the extent that any of these records are maintained electronically make sure that they are password protected and backed up. Ensure your list of user names and passwords is kept safely.
4. What was your experience and what did you learn by gathering your documents?

To do:	By when:

YOUR NOTES, COMMENTS AND ACTIONS

Chapter 2:
Stewardship Basics

KEY VERSE

"The earth is the Lord's, and everything in it."

Psalm 24:1

END TIMES PLANNING IS A CHALLENGE FOR SO MANY

As the founder of a professional services firm in Bristol I served over 800 clients during the 16 years I was in the accountancy business. Most clients did not have a Will and neither did they have adequate life insurance. Planning a funeral service was not a responsibility they even contemplated.

Life is to be lived and the thought of dying is so often a matter to be postponed, and postponed and postponed. Although I think I earned 'nagging rights' with my clients I have to admit that much of my counsel fell on deaf ears. This was the 1980s, a period of growth and opportunity. The families of my clients were mostly young so not even advising them to start a pension scheme was necessarily planning that my clients wished to contemplate.

But over the years I managed to position myself as a financial advisor and was involved in setting up retirement plans for about 30 per cent of my clients.

But what about their Wills? As an accountant I did not have the expertise to write a Will but was able to persuade clients to visit a solicitor when I said to them, "Do you know that if you and your spouse die when the children are young it will be Social Services and the Courts that decide who looks after your children?"

That was enough to persuade many of my clients to visit a solicitor and make their Will. But making that decision regarding the children involved *three* key steps: *Firstly,* for the parents to decide who to nominate as Guardian? *Secondly* for the nominees to accept this responsibility and *thirdly* I always encouraged my clients to take out an insurance policy to cover the additional costs the Guardians would incur. That could include a larger home, education costs, holiday costs, clothing, pocket money and so on. We will look again at matters concerning the appointment of Guardians in chapter three of this study.

I found that for most of my clients using the Will for inheritance tax planning was of little interest. Neither were clients overly bothered about dying intestate (not having a Will) and their estate being subject to the intestacy rules. Except to say that the Will enables you to decide what happens to all that hard-earned wealth and not the State using some very arbitrary and probably inappropriate rules. More about these rules later.

I had to accept that this area of planning was not top of any ones 'to do' list but I was determined to use my professional relationship with clients to influence them where I could. I had been close to too many situations like Mary and family to know that death comes to all, sometimes much sooner than expected. But even in advanced years, planning is massively important as it relieves the burden and stress from younger family members at a time when they are seeking to come to terms with their loss and grief.

I firmly believe that this area of planning is important. I also believe it is a responsibility not to be side stepped or deferred "until a more convenient time."

This study seeks to help with some necessary and recommended practical planning as well as looking at what wisdom and guidance we can gain from the Bible. With over 2350 verses that look at the handling of money and possessions what pointers, what instructions are there within the 66 books that comprise God's Word?

GOD OWNS EVERYTHING

Psalm 24: 1
"The earth is the Lord's, and everything in it, the world, and all who live in it."

Deuteronomy 10:14
"To the Lord your God belong the heavens, even the highest heavens, the earth and everything in it."

1 Corinthians 10:26
"The earth is the Lord's, and everything in it."

1. What do these verses tell you about God's ownership?

2. How does this perspective of God's ownership change how you handle what He has entrusted to you?

WE ARE ALL STEWARDS

1 Corinthians 4:2
"Now it is required that those who have been given a trust must prove faithful."

3. According to this verse, what is your requirement as a steward?

4. How would you define a steward? Describe how faithful you have been in the handling of money.

SEEK COUNSEL

2 Timothy 3: 16-17
"All Scripture is God-breathed and is useful for teaching, rebuking, correcting and training in righteousness, so that the servant of God may be thoroughly equipped for every good work."

Hebrews 4:12
"For the word of God is alive and active. Sharper than any double-edged sword, it penetrates even to dividing soul and spirit, joints and marrow; it judges the thoughts and attitudes of the heart."

5. To what extent should the Bible serve as your counsellor? Why?

6. Do you consistently read and study the Bible? If not, what prevents you from doing so?

Proverbs: 12:15
"The way of fools seems right to them, but the wise listen to advice."

Proverbs 15:22
"Plans fail for lack of counsel, but with many advisors they succeed."

7. What are some of the benefits of seeking counsel?

8. What are some of the benefits you've experienced from seeking counsel?

9. Is there anything that prevents you from seeking counsel?

Psalm 1: 1-3
"Blessed is the one who does not walk in step with the wicked or stand in the way that sinners take or sit in the company of mockers, but whose delight is in the law of the Lord, and who meditates on his law day and night. That person is like a tree planted by streams of water, which yields its fruit in season and whose leaf does not wither—whatever they do prospers."

10. What type of counsellor should you avoid? What type of person do you think should serve as your counsellor? Why?

HOMEWORK - SESSION 2

GOD OWNS EVERYTHING
To assist in helping recognise God's ownership of possessions, it can be helpful to acknowledge that we consider Him to be the owner of our possessions now. We provide a Deed of Ownership for you to sign to do this - but please note that this is not a legal document in any shape or form! By completing this Deed, you will establish a time when you acknowledge God's ownership.

SET YOUR HOUSE IN ORDER

PRACTICAL APPLICATION 2: COMPLETE THE DEED OF OWNERSHIP

11. Discuss this with your spouse (if you are married).

DEED OF OWNERSHIP

DATE: ....

FROM: .... (name + partner's name)

TO: The Lord Jesus Christ

I (we) transfer ownership of the following possessions to the Lord Jesus Christ and thankfully accept the role of manager of these assets. I will faithfully use them according to the Owner's instructions.

SIGNED: Manager(s) of the Lord's possessions:

(1) ....

(2) ....

Note: This is not a legally binding document. It may take 3 or more months before the heart and mind are aligned with fully recognising that God owns everything.

To do:	By when:

STEWARDSHIP BASICS

12. Did you struggle with relinquishing ownership of anything to the Lord? If so, what was it, and why do you think it is difficult?

13. Discuss how you felt when transferring the ownership of your possessions to the Lord.

14. How do you feel about your financial situation? Has that changed by acknowledging everything you own is God's?

15. How do you feel your financial situation could and, perhaps, should be improved?

PRACTICAL APPLICATION 3: LIST YOUR ADVISERS

We've talked about the importance of using good advisors to help you make wise choices about your finances. Start by making a list of the advisers you already have.

You may wish to record in your document file each of your advisors and their contact details, including:
- Name
- Organisation
- Address
- Phone number
- Mobile number
- Email address
- Nature of advisors' role

Your advisors might include:
- Church leader(s)
- Lawyer/solicitor
- Accountant
- Tax advisor (if different from your accountant)
- Financial advisor
- Insurance agent
- Property agent
- Bank and bank contact
- Stockbroker
- Doctor
- Medical consultant
- Close friend or family member

16. Maybe there is nobody on your list or there are areas where you still need an advisor to assist you. What areas are these? How can you find these people?

17. Have you ever suffered from not seeking counsel or from seeking counsel from the wrong people? What happened?

 **YOUR NOTES, COMMENTS AND ACTIONS**

Chapter 3:
Looking at Family and the Future

KEY VERSE

"But seek first his kingdom and his righteousness, and all these things will be given to you as well."

Matthew 6:33

CASE STUDY 2

Stanley and Rosemary started their married life with very little. They were what is known as baby boomers (those born between 1944 and 1964) – children born to parents in the post war years. Those were the days when the country was rebuilding its infrastructure and soldiers returning from the battlefield were exhausted, relieved but excited to discover what a war-free future looked like. There was optimism even though there was post-war rationing of many essentials. Money was in short supply, but on the other hand there was little to spend it on. The technology boom was hardly even around the corner and white goods had yet to become available. Times were tough but there was optimism in the air. In the ensuing years incomes were steady and perhaps even increasing. By the time children arrived Stanley and Rosemary had become relatively prosperous – at least by the standard of the mid 1950s. Their wealth had increased modestly, and they felt able to enjoy spending more in their middle-aged years, even being able to buy a car.

They attended a couple of evening lectures on Wills and Legacies and that challenged them to consider how their faith, their personal views and what they had been listening to could all come together. Having listened to the two speakers - one a financial advisor and the other a legal specialist in Wills and planning they decided to see what guidance they could find in the Bible. But where to start and would all the pieces of the jigsaw fit together? They weren't sure about their planning, as they knew they did not necessarily see eye to eye on all these matters themselves.

Rosemary was concerned about providing for the children in the event of both of them dying. This was really important to her as both her aunt and uncle had been killed when their car was involved in a fatal accident. That had left her cousins being brought up by other members of the family. But both cousins had been unhappy, and this had affected them greatly in their teenage years. Rosemary knew that it was important to give consideration to this as a possibility.

Meanwhile Stanley was more concerned about how the family was going to manage financially, although they had enjoyed a good standard of living, they had overstretched themselves, finances were tight, and they found themselves in debt. To say that Stanley was worried was something of an understatement.

Luke 14: 28-29
"Suppose one of you wants to build a tower. Won't you first sit down and estimate the cost to see if you have enough money to complete it? For if you lay the foundation and are not able to finish it, everyone who sees it will ridicule you."

1. What do these verses illustrate about examining your financial condition to determine if you have enough money for a future need?

THE BIBLE ON WORRY

Matthew 6:25-26
"Therefore I tell you, do not worry about your life, what you will eat or drink; or about your body, what you will wear. Is not life more than food, and the body more than clothes? Look at the birds of the air; they do not sow or reap or store away in barns, and yet your heavenly Father feeds them. Are you not much more valuable than they?"

Matthew 6:33
"But seek first his kingdom and his righteousness, and all these things will be given to you as well."

2. What do these verses say about worry and the Lord providing for our needs?

PROVIDING FOR THE FAMILY

1 Timothy 5: 4, 8
"But if a widow has children or grandchildren, these should learn first of all to put their religion into practice by caring for their own family and so repaying their parents and grandparents, for this is pleasing to God... Anyone who does not provide for their relatives, and especially for their own household, has denied the faith and is worse than an unbeliever."

3. What do these verses communicate?

4. How does this passage motivate you to ensure those dependant on you will be adequately provided for should you die unexpectedly?

THE WORRIES AND DANGERS THAT CAN ARISE WITH DEBT

2 Kings 4:1-7
"The wife of a man from the company of the prophets cried out to Elisha, 'Your servant my husband is dead, and you know that he revered the Lord. But now his creditor is coming to take my two boys as his slaves.' Elisha replied to her, 'How can I help you? Tell me, what do you have in your house?' 'Your servant has nothing there at all,' she said, 'except a small jar of olive oil.' Elisha said, 'Go round and ask all your neighbours for empty jars. Don't ask for just a few. Then go inside and shut the door behind you and your sons. Pour oil into all the jars, and as each is filled, put it to one side.'

She left him and shut the door behind her and her sons. They brought the jars to her and she kept pouring. When all the jars were full, she said to her son, 'Bring me another one.' But she replied, 'There is not a jar left.' Then the oil stopped flowing. She went and told the man of God, and he said, 'Go, sell the oil and pay your debts. You and your sons can live on what is left.'"

5. Why was the widow in danger of losing her sons? Have you made provision for your family in the event of your death? If not, what should you do?

AN EYE ON THE FUTURE

Psalm 39:4-6
"Show me, Lord, my life's end and the number of my days; let me know how fleeting my life is. You have made my days a mere handbreadth; the span of my years is as nothing before you. Everyone is but a breath, even those who seem secure. Surely everyone goes around like a mere phantom; in vain they rush about, heaping up wealth without knowing whose it will finally be."

6. What does the Bible communicate about the length of life on earth?

Psalm 90: 10,12
"Our days may come to seventy years, or eighty, if our strength endures; yet the best of them are but trouble and sorrow, for they quickly pass, and we fly away… Teach us to number our days, that we may gain a heart of wisdom."

7. Why is it important to number our days?

8. Estimate the number of days you have left on earth. How does this impact your thinking? How will you change the way you handle money?

9. How will you provide for your loved ones?

HOMEWORK – SESSION 3

PRACTICAL APPLICATION 4: FUTURE INCOME NEEDS

Look at your current and future income prospects so that you can plan to meet future needs? For example, are you saving enough for retirement? What might happen if one of you dies while you still have dependent children – is there enough life assurance to provide financial security?

It is important to know your current and estimate [likely] future financial situation so that you can plan to meet future needs.

To do:	By when:

PRACTICAL APPLICATION 5: INSURANCE COVER

Life cover: Prepare a schedule showing how your family would be provided for if you died unexpectedly. If there is a likely shortfall, seek advice on the level of insurance cover you should have. Make sure you look at the cost of term insurance – it is often the cheapest form of cover.

Other cover: Are there any areas of insurance coverage that you need but don't yet have? If so, what prevents you from securing coverage? Make sure you research the best quote – that may not be one with the lowest cost. I always believe in being insured by a company with a name I recognise. Again, seek professional advice.

To do:	By when:

PRACTICAL APPLICATION 6: OVER INSURED?

Are there insurances you have but do not need? Particularly, are there insurances for minor risks that you could cover from your own reserves such as white good appliance failure, etc. Cutting out some of these may give you scope to redeploy those saved premium payments to other more strategic areas.

To do:	By when:

PRACTICAL APPLICATION 7: LASTING POWER OF ATTORNEY

The time for you to make future health care decisions is when you are healthy enough to make them for yourself. There are three basic health care documents that each adult should consider executing. The Lasting Power of Attorney – including financial section and Health and Welfare section and a Living Will.

The Health and Welfare Power of Attorney document creates a nominated person to make decisions over day-to-day healthcare and medical treatments when you are unable to make these decisions for yourself. The person you appoint must agree in writing to the appointment.

The Health and Welfare Lasting Power of Attorney is only actionable after the person loses capacity, not before.

For those who want to determine any 'advance decisions' – e.g., you don't want a particular type of medical treatment in certain situations, if you lose capacity in future – you can make a Living Will. A Living Will identifies the type of care a person does or does not want to receive in the event that he or she becomes mentally incompetent during a terminal illness or permanently comatose.

To do:	By when:

PRACTICAL APPLICATION 8: LETTER OF WISHES

A Will is a formal legal document which covers what happens to your assets and liabilities when you die and appoints executors to manage the paperwork and Guardians (where appropriate) to be responsible for dependent children.

It is normal practice for any personal decisions to be included in a separate Letter of Wishes (LOW) addressed to the executors. For example, you may wish to leave items such as:

- Jewellery – often a lady might leave personal jewellery to a daughter or daughter in law
- Watches – a gentleman might leave a watch to son or son-in law
- Other personal items that may be allocated to children or grandchildren include:
- Cars, technology equipment, paintings, sporting equipment and so on.

Note: Your executors will still need to include a valuation of these items in the report to HMRC when applying for probate. In particular a formal valuation of possessions with any significant value is normally required.

You may wish to use this letter to go beyond the transfer of items such as listed above. Some use the LOW to include specific instructions.

A simple standard template follows:

> I make this letter in reference to my Will dated (insert date). I would ask you to have regard to my express wishes that follow:
>
> [Your instructions record here]

The LOW is an expression of your desire. Where the executors or trustees have powers then the LOW can only serve as a "please take note advice" when making their decisions. Matters that may be included in a more comprehensive LOW include:
- Funeral wishes
- List of invitees to the funeral

PRACTICAL APPLICATION 9: GUARDIANS FOR CHILDREN

A Guardian is an adult designated in the Will to care for a child in case both parents die before the child reaches adulthood. This is normally referred to as "Testamentary or Guardianship." While this may be uncomfortable or difficult to think about, it is one of the most important decisions you should make as a parent or carer. If you don't appoint a Guardian, the courts will do it for you in conjunction with Social Services. How do you feel about that happening? The judge may appoint someone who does not embrace your values and does not know Jesus as Lord and Saviour.

It is wise to select a Guardian and maybe an alternate Guardian in case your first choice is unable [or unwilling at the time] to serve sometime in the future. Also, it is wise to separate the roles of Guardian of your children and trustee of your finances. This will help keep the Guardian accountable to spend your estate's finances solely for the benefit of your children.

Deciding who is Guardian of your children is often a very difficult and emotional decision. List the possible candidates, and then prayerfully discuss with your spouse the strengths and weaknesses, the pros and cons, of each candidate.

Here are a few things to consider when choosing a Guardian:

- Whose parenting style, values and commitment to Jesus Christ most closely match your own?
- Who is most able to take on the responsibility of caring for children – emotionally and financially?
- Who do your children feel comfortable with?
- Would your children have to move away, and would that pose any problems?
- Does the person you are considering have other children? If so, would your children fit in well with them?
- Would the person have the time and energy to devote to your children?

A guardian can be appointed:
- in a Will; or
- in writing, dated and signed by the person making the appointment. It can also be signed by someone else following the directions of the person making the appointment.

There is no requirement to use a particular form of words. A statement such as, "In accordance with section 5 of the Children Act 1989 I appoint [X] to be the Guardian of my child [Y]" would suffice.

To do:	By when:

PRACTICAL APPLICATION 10: LETTER TO CHILDREN AND/OR GRANDCHILDREN

Is there something that you wish to say from 'beyond the grave'? Some share their last words concerning their faith in Jesus and the importance of following in Jesus' footsteps. It is your final chance to have your opportunity to follow through Paul's counsel to the Thessalonian Christians as recorded in 1 Thessalonians 4: 13-14 "Brothers and sisters, we do not want you to be uninformed about those who sleep in death, so that you do not grieve like the rest of mankind, who have no hope. For we believe that Jesus died and rose again, and so we believe that God will bring with Jesus those who have fallen asleep in Him."

Others share personal moments that were important concerning the person to whom the letter is addressed.

To do:	By when:

But, while I am not suggesting a long list of letters are there others to whom you might wish to write a letter of thanks or appreciation, or encouragement? Just make sure you also express these sentiments now while you are alive!

Personal note. Please understand why I have emphasised that this study does not provide legal advice. What you include in your Will must be personal and specific to your situation, whereas this study only highlights fairly generic principles and ideas. Can these documents be created using an online service? Probably, but I always advocate professional advice for writing a Will over saving money – what costs less initially can often cost more in the long run.

Remember the story of James and Mary?
While James and Mary are fictional names the essence of their story is not. It is a combination of situations I have encountered during my role as accountant, advisor and executor. While there is rarely one solution that fits all, there are key principles that apply. You can take some basic steps in order to ensure that those who have to deal with the death of a loved one do not have their stress and anxiety levels increased through the negligence of the one who has passed away.

PRACTICAL APPLICATION 11: YOUR WILL

Many years ago, the Law Society used to state that only 1 in 7 adults have a Will. More recently it is reported that 1 in 6 adults do not have a Will. I don't know how true these reports are and, frankly, it doesn't really matter. I always used to believe that probably 1 in 7 people don't have a Will that reflects their current wishes. So, first step – make sure your Will is up-to-date and if you don't have one then make having one a priority.

What should your Will include?
As already stated, it is important to seek professional advice as this is only general guidance. Personally, I think this is preferable to trying to write a Will online or using one of those template Wills. The cost of professional advice is minimal when considering the advice and assurance a professional provides.

A husband and wife might wish to have "mirror" Wills that is ones that are [largely] identical other than the change of names.

Letter dated: 4 Jan 1897
This letter was written by Margaret Thornton's great grandmother

My dear dear children

If you get this to read, it will be when your mother is no longer with you but has gone to father and John to wait for you all coming to them.

This is just to tell you that I have asked Uncle Tom and Uncle Brown to be your guardians and you are to look up to them and be guided by them until you are old enough to relieve them of the responsibility. You know how many kind friends we have always had, and I trust you will always have, and my prayer for you all is that you will grow up worthy to be trusted and loved by all.

My darlings, will you try and love each other dearly, and you know how to do that is to love God first. If you love Him and serve Him then I have no fear of you.

Be gentle and kind to one another, thoughtful for all around you, and obedient and loving to whoever may be put in charge over you.

My precious children, I am writing this, just that you may know the heart's desire of your mother given to yourselves – that you may all grow up good soldiers of Jesus Christ is the prayer of your loving Mother.

A record of the appointment of your executors – these are the people who will sort out your estate, pay any tax and distribute assets in accordance with the Will. It is common to appoint two or three executors, but a sole executor is also permissible.

If you have minor children you should consider naming Guardians who agree to be responsible for looking after your children in the event of both parents dying before they reach adulthood. Typically, people appoint one or two people, often a close family member e.g. a sibling or parent.

The Will could include gifts to named individuals such as children, grandchildren, church etc., either of money or of specific assets.

Your Will should include your preference for burial or cremation.

If you want to leave a share of your estate to someone with 'strings attached' you may also wish to create a trust – for example if you would like to leave the use of assets and income to a second spouse but want to ensure the capital eventually goes to your own children on their death - in this case it is important to seek advice.

"The residue." I have been involved in countless meetings where the legal advisor asks about the residue. That is what remains in your estate after deducting the specific bequests and legacies and paying any tax and how this is to be distributed. Most of the Wills I have been involved in simply allocate the residue equally between the children. But that is not always the case. Some allocate according to perceived need. One of the children may be successful and enjoying adequate 'riches'. Another might be more needy. There are three recommended steps in these circumstances:

1. Pray about your decision with regard to the distribution of the residue
2. Come to agreement with your spouse
3. Share your decision in this matter in advance of your death.

WHEREABOUTS OF DOCUMENTS TO REGISTER YOUR DEATH AND OBTAIN PROBATE

In the first chapter we looked at a fairly comprehensive list of documents that you should maintain in order to facilitate easy to access these on the occasion of your death. The following documents will assist your executor in registering your death and obtaining probate.

- NHS medical card
- Birth certificate
- Driving licence
- Council tax bill
- Marriage or civil partnership certificate (if applicable)
- National Insurance numbers for both partners
- Passport
- Proof of address (e.g. utility bill)

The following will be helpful for your executor:
Assets and liabilities schedule (where located), contact details and account numbers. Also include, where applicable.

- Debts
- Life assurance policies
- Pension policies

- Motor vehicle documents
- Hire purchase/credit agreements/leasing/rental agreements
- Self-assessment tax reference details
- Credit/debit cards
- Mortgage details
- Amounts and dates of gifts not necessarily wholly exempt from inheritance tax – i.e. those made in the last 7 years
- Any other information that you consider appropriate

To do:	By when:

REASONS FOR UPDATING AN EXISTING WILL

These include:
- Changing your executors – it is important that you are comfortable with them and that they are still alive!
- Marriage and divorce – getting married invalidates any existing Wills by either party
- New children/grandchildren
- Children reaching the age of 18
- Change in other family relationships
- Death of someone named in your Will
- A change in the circumstances of someone named as an executor, Guardian or trustee
- A significant increase or decrease in the value of your estate
- Changing tax legislation
- Change in assets
- Changes in your views on legacies
- It has been three years or more since you reviewed your Will

To do:	By when:

YOUR NOTES, COMMENTS AND ACTIONS

Chapter 4:
Legacy Planning

KEY VERSE

"These commandments that I give you today are to be on your hearts. Impress them on your children. Talk about them when you sit at home and when you walk along the road, when you lie down and when you get up."

Deuteronomy 6:6-8

When my wife and I decided to look at our planning we spent a few hours documenting our plans and then filed all our end of life plans away – and cried together. I cannot recall for how long for, but I just remember that we held one another and let the tears flow.

The reason we undertook our planning was a desire to avoid our children having to answer the question, "what would Mum/Dad have wanted?" I have sat in enough meetings to know that there is rarely an answer to that question and the lack of certainty and wishing to "do what Mum/Dad would have wanted" is, well, painful. So, we decided to set out our plans – it will not be our decision as to whether or not these are carried out! At least we have been responsible for giving our children the clearest guidance we can.

SHARING YOUR JOURNEY

Psalm 78: 2-4
"I will open my mouth with a parable; I will utter hidden things, things from of old - things we have heard and known, things our ancestors have told us. We will not hide them from their descendants; we will tell the next generation the praiseworthy deeds of the Lord, his power, and the wonders He has done."

1. Why do you think it is important to share your life's journey with your family?

2. What are three of the most important things the Lord has taught you on your spiritual journey?

1 Thessalonians 4:13-14
"Brothers and sisters, we do not want you to be uninformed about those who sleep in death, so that you do not grieve like the rest of mankind, who have no hope. For we believe that Jesus died and rose again, and so we believe that God will bring with Jesus those who have fallen asleep in him."

3. What does this passage say to you?

INHERITANCES

Proverbs 13:22
"A good person leaves an inheritance for their children's children, but a sinner's wealth is stored up for the righteous."

2 Corinthians 12:14
"Now I am ready to visit you for the third time, and I will not be a burden to you, because what I want is not your possessions but you. After all, children should not have to save up for their parents, but parents for their children."

4. Should parents aim to leave a material inheritance to their children? If so, how are you going to implement this principle?

Proverbs 20:21
"An inheritance claimed too soon will not be blessed at the end"

5. Why do you think an inheritance gained quickly may not be a blessing?

Galatians 4: 1-2
"What I am saying is that as long as an heir is under age, he is no different from a slave, although he owns the whole estate. The heir is subject to guardians and trustees until the time set by his father."

6. According to this verse, what caution should parents exercise when their children are not yet adults?

GENEROSITY

2 Corinthians 9:7
"Each of you should give what you have decided in your heart to give, not reluctantly or under compulsion, for God loves a cheerful giver."

7. Are you a cheerful giver? If not how do you think you can become one?

8. Have you made provision in your Will or through a trust for investing in the Lord's work? How did you come to this decision?

9. Have you made provision in your Will or trust for funding the Lord's work? Describe the factors that led to this decision?

10. How much to leave to your church and other ministries?

11. What other ministries/charities do you wish to leave a bequest to?

PLANNING LESSONS FROM ABRAHAM'S FAMILY

Psalm 71:18
"Even when I am old and grey, do not forsake me, my God, till I declare your power to the next generation, your mighty acts to all who are to come."

12. What did you learn from this verse?

13. Why do you think it is important to declare the power and faithfulness of the Lord to the next generation?

Genesis 49: 29-33
"Then he [Abraham] gave them these instructions: 'I am about to be gathered to my people. Bury me with my fathers in the cave in the field of Ephron the Hittite, the cave in the field of Machpelah, near Mamre in Canaan, which Abraham bought along with the field as a burial place from Ephron the Hittite. There Abraham and his wife Sarah were buried, there Isaac and his wife Rebekah were buried, and there I buried Leah. The field and the cave in it were bought from the Hittites.'

When Jacob had finished giving instructions to his sons, he drew his feet up into the bed, breathed his last and was gathered to his people."

14. What did Jacob do to help his family prepare for his death? How might this apply to you?

15. If you have a current Will or trust, do you think you may change it to reflect what you have learned? If so, how?

PLANNING LESSONS FROM ABRAHAM'S FAMILY

SET YOUR HOUSE IN ORDER

ABOUT LEAVING AN INHERITANCE

First, the Bible makes it clear that parents should leave an inheritance to their children and grandchildren. "A good person leaves an inheritance for their children's children."

Paul tells it like this in 2 Corinthians 12:14, "Children should not have to save up for their parents, but parents for their children." Then the Bible issues a powerful warning, "An inheritance claimed too soon, will not be blessed at the end."

We live in days when [mostly] baby boomer parents have provided financial assistance to their children in what may be regarded as "advance inheritances." These advances are made at junctures in their lives when children had a need or expressed a desire - there is of course a difference.

These 'advances', if you will permit me to refer to them as such may have been made:
- To assist with the purchase of transport, e.g. a car
- To provide a deposit toward a house purchase
- To repay a student loan
- To give a start or boost to encourage the saving habit
- Honeymoon costs.

The above list is clearly not comprehensive!

This advance has not always been made from the baby boomer parent's savings. For this, in many cases, is a generation that is [generally] asset rich but cash poor. As a consequence, parents may have had to borrow against their assets (property, pension or other investments) in order to provide assistance.

In addition to this we are all living longer. The capital saved is today generating much lower income than might have been expected prior to the 2008 global financial crisis. The advantage of this to the younger generation is that their mortgage costs are much less as a percentage of income compared to that of their parents. But as a consequence of living longer the older generations' capital has to stretch further and may be required for care in the elder years. Who ever said that financial planning was straightforward!

Should you leave an inheritance to your grandchildren? And, if so, do not forget to take into account that there may be more on their way in the ensuing years. So, following the direction of the Bible needs prayerful consideration and, ideally, for both spouses to be on the same page with this aspect of planning.

CASE STUDY 3

For a number of reasons Jeremy did not wish to leave all his money immediately to his children. Were there reasons? Oh yes. Reasons that surfaced time and time again during conversations over 20 or more years. Sadly, he died at an early age and very unexpectedly. Even today the annual meetings I have with the family nearly always end up with us all saying that this is what Jeremy would have wanted. Indeed, the two children recognise me as having the mind of their father when it comes to money – which is a privilege I ensure I never abuse. With mirror Wills, all the [substantial] wealth that Jeremy had accumulated passed to his wife – who has very little financial acumen. So, year by year we meet and from time to time the children advance reasons why they would like an 'on account' transfer of their inheritance. As it happens, I have found that Helen and the two children have managed the whole situation extremely well. Jeremy was worried about the potentially damaging effect on his two children of inheriting such a large amount of capital as it concerned him that it could be potentially damaging. All I can add is that they have, all of them have done so very well - Jeremy would have every right to be proud of them all.

Let's look first at three decisions in relation to your heirs...

1. Decide to train your heirs

   The younger generation needs to be given the opportunity to develop financial experience and wisdom before they can be expected to handle an inheritance well. Parenting includes training your children how to handle money wisely. Being in debt does not disqualify you from giving your children good counsel. There is a sense in which maybe it helps you qualify. Remember that the world is all too ready to train your children how to handle money – they have so many ways to help them spend, spend, spend. And the money they spend may well be debt-driven. That spending includes gambling – there are so many football teams sponsored by online betting companies. And then there is all the online and TV advertising. Nightmare!

2. Decide how much to give your heirs

   As discussed in an earlier chapter the traditional approach to estate planning is to make certain specific bequests and then divide the remainder equally between the immediate family. Nothing wrong with that. But maybe this study will assist in exploring and clarifying your planning options. It is, I understand, a huge issue – and this can be especially true where blended families are concerned.

   Pray, and seek counsel. If you are married, discuss this with your spouse

   The amount left may be different per child; and that is not always an easy step to action. We are to love our children equally, which often means helping them uniquely. They are unique not only in their values, commitment to Christ, and ability to deal with life, but also in their vocation, health, and immediate family situation. These circumstances may influence how much you plan to leave each child, and as circumstances change, you may need to adjust your plan.

   Leaving unequal amounts may be a difficult decision because it feels unfair. We simply encourage you to ask for the Lord's guidance if you need to consider such action.

3. Decide when to transfer

   The first two decisions of "to whom" and "how much" pave the way for the decision of "when". You may wish to consider making provision in your estate planning for distributing an inheritance to younger family members over several years, or at an age when you expect or find them to be mature enough to handle the responsibility. I have been involved in establishing any number of trusts for minor children and grandchildren and been around long enough to see them access these funds for expenditures such as home purchase. I have also known children who have simply said, "I'm not interested!" But I suspect they will be one day. Select those you trust (often, indeed normally, this is the child's parents) to appoint as trustees to supervise their use of the funds.

"What I am saying is that as long as an heir is underage, he is no different from a slave, although he owns the whole estate. The heir is subject to Guardians and trustees until the time set by his father" (Galatians 4: 1-2).

SET YOUR HOUSE IN ORDER

HOMEWORK – SESSION 4

PRACTICAL APPLICATION 12: PERSONAL LEGACY

Write a letter, compose a picture album or make a video sharing your family history and milestones in your life with Christ.

To do:	By when:

PRACTICAL APPLICATION 13: FUNERAL INSTRUCTIONS

Remember our first case study? Help your family by providing them with some funeral guidelines:

These are the wishes of: ....

Funeral director preference ....

Location of service ....

Requests for funeral service ....

Name of Minister/Pastor ....

Description of service ....

....

Musical selections ....

Special requests: biblical passage, speakers etc. ....

Cemetery if appropriate ....

Specific request re burial/cremation ....

Pallbearer request (if any)

Type of casket ....

Memorial: ....

Flowers Yes/No

If in lieu of flowers please make contributions to the following organisations:

1. ....

2. ....

3. ....

Signed .... Dated ....

PRACTICAL APPLICATION 14: TESTIMONY LETTER

One powerful way to describe to your loved ones and the next generation the faithfulness of the Lord, is to include your testimony in a separate document accompanying your Will. Here is an example:

"I wish to encourage my family friends and loved ones with the promises of the Lord. At the age of 14, I started a personal relationship with Jesus Christ, my Lord and Saviour. I can assure you that over the years I have learnt to have complete confidence and trust in Him and that I received the gift of eternal life because Jesus died on the cross for the forgiveness of all my sins. The Bible puts it like this in John 3:16: "For God so loved the world that He gave His one and only Son, that whoever believes in Him shall not perish but have eternal life."

As King Solomon said in Ecclesiastes 3: 1-2, "There is a time for everything, and a season for every activity under the heavens: a time to be born and a time to die." As a follower of Jesus, I am not afraid to die. Paul wrote in his letter to the Church in Philippi, "For to me, to live is Christ and to die is gain" (Philippians 1:21). And again, the same writer wrote in 2 Corinthians 5:8, "to be absent from the body, is to be present with the Lord (KJV).

"I desire to remind you that those who know Christ as their Saviour never have to say good-bye! Our grief is temporary; therefore I don't want you to grieve as do the rest who have no hope." (2 Thessalonians 4: 1,3). Rejoice with me! I am finally Home. Jesus told us, "I am the resurrection and the life; he who believes in Me will live even if he dies" (John 11:25). I am alive with Jesus! And for those of you who have put your faith and trust in Jesus, we share the destiny of Heaven, and I am looking forward, one day, to our eternal reunion. For those of you who haven't yet put their faith and trust in Christ, my heart yearns to think that we will be separated forever. Please trust Him as you Lord and Saviour, today."

To do:	By when:

DYING WITHOUT A WILL OR WITHOUT A VALID WILL

Following on from our last study when we considered some essential aspects of a Will we will look now at what happens when there is no Will. However, before we look at this please allow me to state that you really don't wish to die intestate. Let's look at this in a little more detail.

While there are various surveys that indicate that more than 60 per cent of adults do not have a Will I cannot find any reliable statistics that indicate how many people actually die without having made a Will. There is a difference!

The Eastern Daily Press reported in 2017 that 86 people had died without having made a Will and have an unclaimed estate. Which doesn't really tell you very much. However, visit the Government's website of unclaimed estates and there are thousands.

The Office for National Statistics was asked:
1. How many people died intestate last year in the UK?
2. How much revenue the government received from those intestate deaths?
3. How is this money spent and on whom?

They replied:

Thank you for your enquiry.
Unfortunately, we only hold information recorded in connection with registering the death, which does not include any information relating to the administration of their estate.

In 2018 The Daily Telegraph reported that, "More than £1 million has passed to the Prince of Wales's Duchy of Cornwall estate in the last six years from people who died without making a Will or having an heir.

Under powers dating back to medieval times, the Duchy is entitled to all unclaimed property and estates left when someone dies in Cornwall, in an arrangement known as *bona vacantia*.

In the last financial year alone, £552,000 passed to the Duchy under the ancient law, which was put in place when the Duchy was created by Edward III in 1337 for his son and heir, Edward, the Black Prince.

The Prince of Wales does not, however, keep any of the money; instead it is distributed in charitable donations through the Duke of Cornwall's Benevolent Fund, with a small amount kept in reserve for any future claims on unclaimed estates."

The waters look a little muddy on the actuality of those who have died intestate, but the rules are crystal clear.

INTESTACY RULES

In England and Wales:
If there are surviving children, grandchildren or great grandchildren, the spouse or civil partner will inherit

- All the personal property and belongings of the person who has died, and
- The first £250,000 of the estate, and
- Half (only) of the remaining estate.

In Scotland:
Where there is a surviving spouse only, they receive the entire estate. However, where children, parents or brothers and sisters of the deceased survive the surviving spouse receives:

- The interest in their house up to £473,000. If the house has a greater value then a cash alternative is available
- Furniture and household goods up to £29,000
- A legacy of £50,000 if there are children or £89,000 otherwise.

The balance of the estate is shared between the children if there are any, and between the parents and siblings (including their surviving children if siblings have pre-deceased) if there are no children.

In Northern Ireland:
Legacies of £250,000 as above for England and Wales.

If there are children surviving, the surviving spouse or civil partner take:

1. The personal chattels absolutely
2. The legacy as above free of inheritance tax and costs, with interest at 6% per annum from the date of death, and
3. An absolute interest in one-half of the residue of the estate, where only one child of the intestate also survives
4. An absolute interest in one-third of the residue of the estate, where more than one child of the intestate also survives.

If a child of the intestate predeceases him/her leaving issue who survive the intestate, the surviving spouse or civil partner takes the same share as if that child had survived the intestate.

Please note that jointly held assets such as joint bank accounts and property held under joint tenancy will automatically pass to the surviving owner outside of any Will or the intestacy rules

If you are in a blended family your new spouse could inherit everything leaving your own children with nothing.

CASE STUDY 4

For example, take John and Claire who live in England and remarried two years ago and have not written Wills since then. They each have two children from previous relationships, all under 18. They have bought a house worth £400,000 together with a small mortgage. Most of the house purchase cost was contributed by John from a previous house sale and from money inherited by his parents. John has £200,000 of savings in ISAs.

If John were to die suddenly, Claire would inherit the house automatically and up to £250,000 of other assets so in effect would inherit everything. She would have no obligation to share any assets with John's children but also would have no rights to keep John's children if their mother was still alive.

CASE STUDY 5

In another example, Sue is a lady in her 50s. She separated from her husband two years ago but they are not yet divorced. She had no Will. She has a property worth £500,000 which she bought outright using savings and money inherited from her parents. She would like to leave it to her sister and sister's children but if she dies the first £250,000 plus half the balance will go to her separated husband.

And finally...
Other circumstances lead to different allocations. If there are no surviving relatives, the estate passes to the Crown!

I know of no one that wishes to see their hard-earned capital distributed in such an arbitrary way, or for it to go to the Crown.

WHY PEOPLE DON'T MAKE A WILL?

There are a number of reasons including:

- It's just not a priority – "I must get around to it sometime". But sometime never seems to arrive
- Some report that they think they are going to "jinx themselves"
- Facing and resolving the issue of guardianship in the event of both parents' death
- The inability to agree or make a decision in a blended family situation (where partners have children from different marriages/relationships).

DISTRIBUTION OF PERSONAL PROPERTY

One of the biggest areas of conflict among heirs is items that may have little value if sold to others but have enormous sentimental value and importance to surviving family members.

To help minimise the potential discord among heirs, it can be helpful for you to choose how you wish to have some of your personal property to be distributed. After making your decision, this should be included in a Letter of Wishes and added to your Will documentation as instructions to your executors – note this is not normally included as a specific clause in the Will.

Beneficiary	Item

For the avoidance of doubt it would be advisable to take a photograph of each specific item. This list should be reviewed regularly and updated if items are sold or given away.

LEGACY PLANNING

A NOTE TO THE MAIN BREADWINNER

CASE STUDY 6 AND [MAYBE OUR FINAL PRACTICAL APPLICATION 15]

What you read here may not be applicable to you, but suffice to say that it was for my wife and me and for a good many of my accounting firm clients.

Setting the scene – an exert from my own personal journey:
If you are the main earner in the household and something were to happen to you what would be the financial impact? I am for this purpose excluding the massive emotional impact and the impact on work/business implications. You may have dependent children and your spouse may well have to provide for them. This may continue on beyond the age of 18. What about the cost of higher education? There are often reports of the massive debt that students have when they leave University.

I started an accountancy business in my late twenties and was successful in attracting many young business owners as clients. I had children, as did most of my clients. Here is a précis of how I looked at my own family situation and also, I gave my client's similar counsel.

In my case I was the primary family earner. My wife was responsible for looking after the three children. She did not need to work, as I was fortunate in being able to provide for our financial needs. Notwithstanding that she was often found doing a wide range of jobs – "whatever needs doing I will do," she used to say.

But I thought through the situation my wife would be in if something were to happen to me. The Building Society had insisted that I take out life cover so that the mortgage would be paid off in the event of my death, but that was the total sum of my planning at that point.

I sat down to work out what it might cost to bring up all my children to the age of 18. I included all the costs I could think of; housekeeping, property costs, holidays, transport, education, gifts and so on. I then added in some capital for my wife to access for her living costs beyond the children leaving home. Having added it all up I sought advice on the best form of life cover. I was advised to take out a decreasing term insurance policy. Now, you know that the purpose of this study is never to 'sell insurance' or give advice but just to give you one example. I asked for a quote from an online comparison website. The input data was:

Age: 30
Gender: Male
Amount: £1,000,000
Decreasing term: 20 years

The quote I received from a well-known and established company was less than £22 per month for 20 years. That monthly amount will effectively reduce in relative cost as inflation impacts its true cost - and incomes will [hopefully] rise during that time.

Why did I do this? I was committed to providing for my family and ensuring that I did not add to the burden of my wife in not only having to bring the children up single handedly but also to provide for them financially. I grew up in a single parent household and I saw my Mother struggle. No way was I prepared to see history repeat itself. Besides, I had promised to: "have and to hold from this day forward, for better for worse, for richer for poorer (I decided that leaving my wife poor was not a godly option), in sickness and in health, to love and to cherish, until death us do part" That wasn't good enough for me I was committed to providing for her and our family beyond the grave!

For me personally, two things followed on from that promise:
- that leaving my wife poor was not a godly option, and
- That I should commit to providing for her and our dependent family from beyond my grave!

To do:	By when:

 ## YOUR NOTES, COMMENTS AND ACTIONS

LEGACY PLANNING

SUMMARY OF YOUR ACTIONS

You may wish to summarise your key thoughts and actions with a date for the action point to be completed.

Action point No.	Action	Date I plan to have this completed	Completed
1			
2			
3			
4			
5			
6			
7			
8			
9			
10			

Appendix

TECHNICAL TERMS EXPLAINED

Note: Throughout we use the upper case for a Will, while most others use lower case. This is purely personal preference to distinguish from the use of the word as a verb.

This is a selection of some of the terms that may be used in matters relating to this study and in estate planning matters. It is not comprehensive.

Asset
Anything a person owns that has value.

Beneficiary
The title given to those who benefit from the estate. These people or organisations will be named in the Will.

Bequest
A gift left to a person, organisation or charity in a Will.

Blended family
A blended family is one where the parents have children from previous relationships but all the members come together as one unit.

Civil partnership
An officially registered civil partnership between two same-sex partners gives the civil partners the same rights as a married couple.

Codicil
The name given to a document that changes a Will. It must be properly executed and witnessed.

Deceased
One who has died.

Estate planning
The process of anticipating and arranging, during a person's life, for the management and disposal of that person's estate during the person's life and at and after their death.

Executor
A person or persons named in a Will or Codicil to be the personal representative in the administration of the estate. It is the executor's responsibility to apply for probate.

Exemption
Certain gifts and transfers are exempt from inheritance tax (e.g. gifts to a spouse or to charities).

Family trust
A Trust established during your lifetime designed to prevent any formal administration being necessary upon death. The Trust can also simplify generation skipping or protection measures.

Inheritance tax
The tax due on the estate. Tax is payable at 40% (this may be reduced subject to gifts given to charity to 36%) after exemptions have been deducted. Professional advice should be sought to review the estate plan regarding its effectiveness in reducing liability to this tax.

Gift
A transfer from one individual to another without fair compensation.

Inheritance
The assets received from someone who has died.

Intestacy
The distribution of estate assets when the person dies without a Will. In intestacy, a court with jurisdiction over property in the estate distributes a deceased person's assets by applying a single, one-size-fits-all formula. This is done according to the law of intestacy and depends on which British country's jurisdiction applies. A person who dies without a Will is said to be "intestate."

Lasting power of attorney (LPA)
Allows you to give someone you trust the legal power to make decisions on your behalf in case you later become unable to make decisions for yourself. The person who makes the LPA is known as the 'donor' and the person given the power to make decisions is known as the 'attorney'.

Lasting power of attorney for health and welfare
Covers decisions about health and personal welfare.

Lifetime gift
Something you give away while you are alive rather than by your Will.

Living Will
A written document that states you do not wish to be kept alive by artificial means when the illness or injury is terminal.

Medical certificate
A certificate issued by a doctor showing the cause of death. The medical certificate is needed to register a death.

Mirror Will
A set of two Will documents that are similar in content. Such documents are normally written for 'couples'.

Net estate
The value of an estate after all debts have been paid. (Inheritance tax is based on the net value of an estate.)

Personal representative
Another name for an executor or administrator.

Power of attorney
A legal document that authorises a person to act on another's behalf for specific purposes and under specific conditions.

Probate
The legal process of validating a Will, paying debts, and distributing assets after death.

Rules of intestacy
The rules that set out who inherits if someone dies without leaving a valid Will.

Settlor
The person who sets up a Trust.

Spouse
Husband or wife.

Testator
The person making a Will.

Trust
Generally, a trust is a legal mechanism in which property is held by one person or entity (the "trustee") for the benefit of another person or persons (the "beneficiaries") pursuant to the terms of a written trust agreement. There are many different kinds of trusts.

Will
A legally executed document that explains how a person wants his or her property distributed after death.

Witnesses
Two independent people who are required to sign the Will stating that they have observed the Testator signing it. The witnesses must not be benefiting from the Will or be married to (or be in a civil partnership with) anyone benefiting from the Will.

PAGES FOR YOUR USE

The following pages contain one page versions of the checklists in the study manual.

YOUR DOCUMENTS

Are your documents organised? Here is a list of possibly relevant documents that you might have in your document filing system. Select as applicable to your circumstances:

Bank accounts
Birth certificate
Car registration certificate
Citizenship papers
Company shareholders (or business) agreements
Debt papers e.g. loans; hire purchase, leasing
Deeds
Divorce decree
Funeral wishes including invitees, service preferences
Insurance policies
Investments including Premium Bonds; shares; ISAs; securitised investments etc.
Lasting power of attorney including health and welfare
Leases
Letter of wishes
Marriage certificate
Mortgage(s)
National insurance details
Online files, including user name and passwords
Passport
Pension policies
Professional advisors
Retirement papers – not covered by any other point on this list
Schedule of assets
Self-assessment tax returns
Trusts
User names and passwords (all - very important)
Wills including any deeds of variation

NOTES

- Some of the above may not be appropriate but I am sure you can work them out according to your own circumstances.
- Original documents should be your first choice but failing that then a photocopy.
- To the extent that any of these records are maintained electronically make sure that they are password protected and backed up. Ensure your list of user names and passwords is kept safely.

LIST OF ADVISORS

Who are your advisors? You may wish to record in your document file each of your advisors and their contact details, including:

Name
Organisation
Address
Phone number
Mobile number
Email address
Nature of advisors' role

Your advisors:
Church leader(s)
Lawyer/solicitor
Accountant
Tax advisor (if different from your accountant)
Financial advisor
Insurance agent
Property agent
Bank and bank contact
Stockbroker
Doctor
Medical consultant

....

....

....

....

FUNERAL INSTRUCTIONS

These are the wishes of: ....

Funeral director preference ....

Location of service ....

Requests for funeral service ....

Name of Minister/Pastor ....

Description of service ....

....

Musical selections ....

Special requests: biblical passage, speakers etc ....

Cemetery if appropriate ....

Specific request re burial/cremation ....

Pallbearer request (if any)

Type of casket ....

Memorial: ....

Flowers Yes/No

If in lieu of flowers please make contributions to the following organisations:

1. ....

2. ....

3. ....

Signed .... Dated ....

DISTRIBUTION OF PERSONAL PROPERTY

One of the biggest areas of conflict among heirs is items that may have little value if sold to others but have enormous sentimental value and importance to surviving family members.

To help minimise the potential discord among heirs, it can be helpful for you to choose how you wish some of your personal property distributed. After making your selection, this should be included in a letter of wishes and added to your Will documentation as instructions to your Executors – note this is not normally included as a specific clause in the Will.

Beneficiary	Item
....	....
....	....
....	....
....	....
....	....
....	....
....	....
....	....
....	....
....	....
....	....
....	....
....	....
....	....
....	....

For avoidance of doubt it would be advisable to take a photograph of each specific item.

SOME THOUGHTS ON INHERITANCE TAX PLANNING

Planning to minimise the liability to IHT is a team effort involving you and your professional adviser. These notes are based on the tax year 2019/20 that is from 6 April 2019 to 5 April 2020.

To enable long-term planning to be set in place, it is important to carefully consider your planning options before making decisions about your financial planning and the distribution of your estate.

It is possible to transfer unused nil-rate band allowances between spouses or civil partners. These rules apply to allow a claim to be made to transfer any unused IHT nil-rate band on a person's death from the estate of their deceased spouse/civil partner.

The amount of the nil rate-band potentially available for transfer will be based on the proportion of the nil-rate band unused when the first spouse or civil partner died. If on the first death the chargeable estate is £150,000 and the nil-rate band is £300,000, then 50% of the nil-rate band is unused. If the nil rate band when the surviving spouse dies is £350,000, then that would be increased by 50% to £525,000.

MAIN RESIDENCE AND THE NIL-RATE BAND

There is a residence nil-rate band for an estate if the deceased's interest in a residential property, which has been their residence at some point and is included in their estate, is left to one or more direct descendants on death.

The value of the main residence nil-rate band for an estate will be the lower of the net value of the interest in the residential property (after deducting any liabilities such as mortgage) or the maximum amount of the band. The maximum amount will be phased in as follows:

- £100,000 for 2017 to 2018
- £125,000 for 2018 to 2019
- £150,000 for 2019 to 2020
- £175,000 for 2020 to 2021.

It will then increase in line with CPI for subsequent years. However, the amount is tapered if the total value of the estate exceeds £2 million, and falls to nil where the value of the estate exceeds £2.3 million in 2019/20.

There is also relief if the deceased has downsized during their life and thus the value of the home at date of death is lower than the nil-rate band residential enhancement. In that case it is possible to add other assets into the nil-rate band provided they are left to direct descendants on death.

Any unused nil-rate band will be transferred to a surviving spouse or civil partner. When added to the £650,000 existing nil-rate band (2 x £325,000) this could provide a total nil-rate band of £1 million for a married couple or civil partners.

WHEN SHOULD I PLAN FOR IHT?

Now! IHT is currently payable where generally a person's (IHT-taxable) wealth is in excess of £325,000 until the tax year 2020/21. Thus, if you own your own house and have some savings, life assurance policies, or business assets, your estate could be liable.

WHY NOW?

Most gifts made during your lifetime will be entirely exempt from IHT if you live for seven years after making the gift.

HOW DOES IHT WORK?

When you die, IHT will be charged on your personal wealth, together with all or a proportion of your lifetime gifts made in the preceding seven years.

The full rate of tax is 40%, but this is reduced on a sliding scale for gifts made between three and seven years before your death. If you make substantial bequests to charity, not only are these exempt from IHT but they can also affect the rate paid on the remainder of your estate. To benefit you must leave at least 10% of your estate to charity, which can reduce the estate rate to 36%.

WHAT DO I NEED TO CONSIDER?

You must think about the following:
1. The value of your assets now, and how this may change with the effluxion of time
2. Your own financial security
3. Your family's future needs

WHAT ABOUT MY FINANCIAL SECURITY?

You need to make sure that you and your spouse are properly provided for, particularly in retirement. It would not make sense to give assets to your children only to find that in later life you need to ask for some or all of them back!

AND WHAT ABOUT MY FAMILY?

You need to think about what degree of control you would want your children to have over any assets you may transfer to them.

You also need to work out how much your spouse would need if you were to die first. This would, of course, have to be reflected in your Will.

In addition, you need to find out the intentions of parents or elderly relatives about their own assets.

HOW DOES IHT AFFECT MY BUSINESS?

In general, a business you control will attract business property relief of 100%. In other words, your business can be passed on with no IHT being paid.

Assets owned by you but used by a partnership in which you are a partner, or a company you control, attract business property relief of 50%.

Similar reliefs apply to agricultural property.

WHAT CAN I DO TO REDUCE THE IHT BILL?

1. Transfers of assets between spouses and civil partners are exempt from IHT, but other lifetime gifts may be more tax-efficient.
2. Lifetime gifts are potentially exempt from IHT, and there is no limit on such transfers, so this is an excellent way of transferring assets that you do not need to keep in your estate. It may be advisable to cover substantial gifts by insurance against death within seven years.
3. Trusts let you transfer assets out of your estate for IHT purposes, but enable trustees to exercise some degree of control over the capital or income (and you can be a trustee). There may be an IHT charge, but this would be at 20%, and then only if the transfer is over £325,000.
4. Life assurance policies (unless designed to cover IHT liabilities) should be assigned during your lifetime so that the proceeds do not form part of your estate on death. The most common assignees are spouses, family members, and trusts.